Jesus' 30 recorded healings are retold in the following books:

Jesus' Healings, Part 1

Man Healed of Mental Illness (Capernaum)
Peter's Mother-in-Law Healed of Fever
Man Healed of Leprosy
Man Healed of Paralysis
Man with Withered Hand Healed
Nobleman's Son Healed of Illness
Centurion's Servant Healed of Paralysis
Widow's Son Brought Back to Life
Woman Healed of Sin
Man Healed of Blindness and Dumbness

Jesus' Healings, Part 2

Man Healed of Mental Illness (Gadara)
Jairus' Daughter Brought Back to Life
Woman Healed of Illness
Two Men Healed of Blindness
Man Healed of Dumbness
Man Healed of Disability
Woman's Daughter Healed of Illness
Man Healed of Deafness and Speech Problems
Man Healed of Blindness
Man's Son Healed of Epilepsy

Jesus' Healings, Part 3

Woman Healed of Back Problem
Man Healed of Swelling
Ten Men Healed of Leprosy
Woman Healed of Adultery
Man Healed of Blindness from Birth
Lazarus Brought Back to Life
Bartimaeus Healed of Blindness
Zacchaeus Healed of Dishonesty
Malchus' Ear Healed
Jesus' Resurrection

Other products by the authors and illustrator include the following:

- Ten Commandments Cards
- Beatitudes Cards
- Interactive Bible Time-Line

Jesus' healings
Part 3

Written by

Mary Jo Beebe
Olene E. Carroll
Nancy H. Fischer

Illustrated by

Genevieve Meek

Table of Contents

**GENERAL PUBLICATIONS
BIBLE PRODUCTS, CSPS**
Boston, Massachusetts, U.S.A.

ISBN: 87510-404-5

Introduction

About the Book

Jesus' Healings, Part 3, is the third in a three-part series. The three books are written for all ages—children, teenagers, and adults—anyone who is interested in the great healing work of Jesus.

All 30 of Jesus' Healings Included

The three books bring to life in simple language the 30 recorded healings of Christ Jesus. These healings span a period of possibly three years in Jesus' life. They include healings of sickness and sin, as well as four accounts of restoring life, one of them being Jesus' own resurrection.

Stories Arranged in Chronological Order

We have attempted to place the healings in chronological order according to Bible scholars. Not one of the Gospel writers includes all 30 of the healings. Some of the stories are found in only one Gospel book. In some cases, stories can be found in two of the books, sometimes in three, and two of them in all four. As a result, no exact chronology is known.

Account Chosen Based on Detail

When more than one account of a healing story occurs, in most cases we have chosen the account that is the richest in detail. When there are significant details in another account, we have added that information in sidebars.

Stories—Self-Contained

Each of the healing stories in the book is self-contained, with references to other pages in the book for definitions and commentary. While this feature is helpful for reading and studying individual stories, we recommend that you take the time to read the book from beginning to end as well. This will give you a full and inspired understanding of the scope and importance of Jesus' healings.

Written in Simple Language

The stories are written in contemporary English and at a level young children can understand. Sidebars provide additional information and commentary about the stories that will be interesting to older children and adults. In a few of the stories, passages too difficult for young children to understand have been placed in sidebars.

While every attempt has been made to write the stories in simple language, some stories may still be beyond the understanding of very young children. Parents and teachers must use their own discretion about the appropriateness of stories. In some cases, it may be helpful to paraphrase a story or leave out certain sections.

Details and Ideas Added for Understanding

In writing the stories, we have added details and ideas with the intent of making the stories more understandable. The details are supported by authoritative Bible scholars. You can find sources in the bibliography on page 59.

Based on Concepts in the Bible and *Science and Health with Key to the Scriptures*

In the healing stories, we have identified spiritual truths that were the foundation of Jesus' healings. These truths are based on concepts found in the Bible and in *Science and Health with Key to the Scriptures* by Mary Baker Eddy. *Science and Health* provides inspiring insights into the Scriptures, helping the reader recognize the spiritual ideas that were so important in Jesus' healings. These include Jesus' spiritual understanding of God, which enabled him to see beyond the material senses and to affirm the spiritual reality.

Introduction

Special Features of the Book

Jesus' Healings includes features you may want to explore before you read the stories. Understanding how the book is organized and arranged will enhance your enjoyment of it.

Sidebars like this provide information about a bolded word or phrase in the story.

Sidebars like this provide commentary or information from another Gospel account. The sidebar color matches a colored square in the story for easy reference.

Sidebars like this show where information can be found in another story about a bolded word or phrase in the story.

NOTE: All Bible quotations in sidebars are from the King James Version.

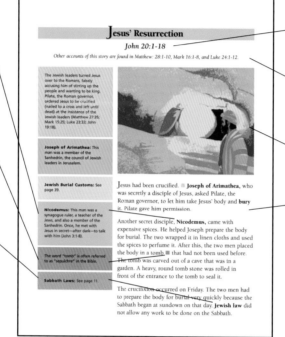

Bible book and verses where the story can be found.

Bible books and verses where other accounts of the story can be found.

Illustrations enhance children's (and adults') understanding and enjoyment of the stories.

The text is easily read and understood by all ages.

The end of each story is indicated by a large colored square.

Bible verse sidebars provide a Bible verse with spiritual truths that Jesus would have known—also comments about the practicality of these truths to heal today.

The "What Can YOU Do?" sidebars provide ideas for children and teens that help them see how they can apply the spiritual truths in the healing story to their lives.

Introduction

Jesus and His Healing Mission

Christ Jesus' healings inspired the people of Palestine in the first century A.D., and they inspire us today. While Jesus' background was humble, his words and works were mighty.

Jesus grew to manhood knowing that his mission was God-directed. Luke reports that at the age of 30, Jesus began his ministry. It was in the synagogue in Nazareth, where he had grown up, that he announced to those who had known him as a child and now as a man, that he had a mission—one that the prophet Isaiah had told them about many years before. He stood to read it,

> The Spirit of the Lord is upon me, because he hath anointed me to preach the gospel to the poor; he hath sent me to heal the brokenhearted, to preach deliverance to the captives, and recovering of sight to the blind, to set at liberty them that are bruised, to preach the acceptable year of the Lord (Luke 4:18, 19).

All eyes were on this gentle, loving man as he told the people that this Scripture was fulfilled that day. They were in the presence of the man who was bringing good news to the world. This message of God's infinite power and love for His children would heal sickness and sin and restore life.

For the next three years, Jesus took this message into the cities and regions of Palestine. Matthew tells us: "And there followed him great multitudes of people from Galilee, and from Decapolis, and from Jerusalem, and from Judæa, and from beyond Jordan" (Matthew 4:25). Although most of Jesus' works occurred in Galilee, he also healed in other regions, such as Samaria and Phoenicia in Syria. "Beyond Jordan" refers to the regions to the east of the Jordan River that included Decapolis, Perea, and Gaulanitis.

He taught, he preached, he healed the sick and sinning, and he brought people back to life. The Bible records 30 individual healings. But it also tells us that Jesus healed many others. Here, Matthew tells of Jesus healing large numbers of people,

> And great multitudes came unto him, having with them those that were lame, blind, dumb, maimed, and many others, and cast them down at Jesus' feet; and he healed them: insomuch that the multitude wondered, when they saw the dumb to speak, the maimed to be whole, the lame to walk, and the blind to see: and they glorified the God of Israel (Matthew 15:30, 31).

Jesus sent out his closest disciples (as well as 70 others) to heal as he did. He told them,

> And as ye go, preach, saying, The kingdom of heaven is at hand. Heal the sick, cleanse the lepers, raise the dead, cast out devils: freely ye have received, freely give (Matthew 10:8).

And Jesus didn't leave his instruction to heal only with his disciples. It's clear that he expected all of his followers down through the ages to heal through spiritual means. He said,

> Verily, verily, I say unto you, He that believeth on me, the works that I do shall he do also; and greater works than these shall he do (John 14:12).

Introduction

Jesus' Times and the Dawn of the Messiah

Jesus was a Jew. His background was grounded in the Jewish belief in one God. He lived in a time when the Jews had very little control over their own lives. Many years before Jesus' time, Palestine was conquered by the Greeks. During that period, the Greeks tried to destroy the Jewish religion. Life for the Jews was extremely harsh. In 63 B.C. the Romans took over Palestine, and the Jews felt the enormous weight of that rule.

The major religious leaders of their times, referred to in the Bible as the scribes and Pharisees, developed a system of worship that was centered on everyday human observance of religious laws. Some of these laws were written; others were spoken. The intent of these laws was to help the Jews keep their faith centered in their belief in God. The effect, however, was that the laws were so restrictive and the details so minute that too often people focused on the laws more than on the inspiration and power of God.

This was the political and religious environment in which Jesus began his healing ministry.

Hundreds of years before Jesus' time and during periods of occupation of their lands by other countries, the Jewish people began to develop the idea that a Messiah would come some day to free them from their enemies. Many thought of this Messiah as a king from the family of David (see **Messiah/Christ** on page 5). Many thought of him as a priest. Others spoke of a prophet who would come. Old Testament prophets told of a coming Messiah and what could be expected when he came. In fact, when Jesus read from the prophet Isaiah one Sabbath day in the Nazareth synagogue, the passage was one that the Jews would have recognized as referring to such a Messiah.

But Jesus' idea of a Messiah was a new one. He brought people fresh insights about his mission. He brought them an understanding of the Messiah as a spiritual idea that would heal. This spiritual idea was his and everyone's relationship to God as God's spiritual, perfect children. If one had complete faith in this view of man created in God's image and likeness—whole, healthy, and free—and understood the all-power of God, then they would feel and experience the kingdom of heaven, or harmony. Healing would be the outcome. And Jesus proved this with wonderful, powerful healings. Multitudes of people came to Jesus to be healed. Seeing and experiencing healing, they began to realize that he must be the Messiah they had longed for.

Each step of the way in his ministry, Jesus worked to help the religious leaders and the people understand the concept of the Messiah he was presenting. But Jesus encountered much opposition. He was a threat to the scribes' and Pharisees' system of religion. As they saw it, they were in danger of losing their Jewish following if the people accepted Jesus' teachings.

The scribes and Pharisees were focused on their materialistic system of worship and their need to preserve this system. They refused to recognize Jesus' works as evidence of the Spirit or power of God—the basis of his system of healing. This prevented most of them from seeing the spiritual import of Jesus' teachings and healings. This was an import that blessed the world then and continues to bless as spiritual healing finds its rightful place in the 21st century.

Introduction

The Messiah/Christ concept is central to an understanding of Jesus and his healings. Many of the healing stories that follow will refer to this information about the Messiah/Christ.

Messiah/Christ: The Hebrew word for "Messiah" and the Greek word for "Christ" mean "anointed"—chosen and dedicated—to save or deliver. Many Jews believed the Messiah of the Old Testament was a special anointed king from the family of David, who would come someday. This king, the "Son of David," would get rid of all their enemies and set up a kingdom that would last forever. Other Jews believed the Messiah would be a priest who would purify the way Israel worshiped God. And others saw that a prophet like Moses would come. Isaiah told of a Messiah who would be a light not just for Jews but for the whole world. To the Jews, light was a symbol of God's purity and goodness, which would save people from all their troubles.

Before Jesus' birth, Mary was told by an angel that her son would be great and would be called the Son of the Highest and that God would give him the throne of David. It was said at Jesus' birth that a Saviour, Christ the Lord, was born. John the Baptist prophesied that a Messiah was to come, one who was "mightier" than he.

At the beginning of Jesus' ministry, when he read from Isaiah in the Nazareth synagogue, he declared that he was "anointed" by the Spirit to be the great prophet described in Isaiah, one who would bless all by helping the poor and captives and healing people. Later, when John the Baptist sent his disciples to Jesus to ask him if he was the Messiah, Jesus referred them to his "works"—"the blind see, the lame walk, the lepers are cleansed, the deaf hear, the dead are raised, to the poor the gospel is preached" (Luke 7:22).

Jesus didn't think of himself as an earthly king. He saw his role as fulfilling the scripture to heal and teach and to bring to light the "kingdom of God"—the reign of harmony. He saw the Christ as his—and everyone's—spiritual selfhood. He knew that God created man in His image and likeness and kept him that way. Therefore, man is always spiritual, whole, and complete. Jesus never allowed the material picture of sickness, sin, and death to have power or reality in his thought.

By knowing that the Christ, or his spiritual selfhood, was the only truth or reality, Jesus destroyed the "enemies" of sickness, sin, and death. And this understanding of the Christ brought the "kingdom of God"— complete harmony.

Jesus' life, teachings, and spiritual healings showed how clearly he understood his spiritual selfhood. People began to give him the title of "Christ," calling him "Christ Jesus." Christ Jesus is an example for us all. We, too, can heal as he commanded his followers to do, by understanding God's all-power and our spiritual relationship to Him.

In the recorded stories of Jesus' healings, names that refer to the Messiah are:

Christ
Holy One of God
Prophet
Son of David
Son of the Most High God
Light of the World
Son of God

Woman Healed of Back Problem
Luke 13:10-17

See "Man's Son Healed of Epilepsy," *Jesus' Healings, Part 2,* page 55.

Mount Hermon is in northern Palestine and is the highest mountain in the country (9,100 feet or 2,774 meters).

Jerusalem: Jerusalem was the most important city in Bible times. It is in the center of the country up in the hills of Judea. David captured the city and made it the capital of his kingdom and the center of worship. Solomon built the first Temple here. (See **Temple** on page 26.) For centuries Jews traveled to Jerusalem to festivals held in the Temple. Jerusalem has had a long history of rulers and kings, war and peace, destruction and rebuilding. In Jesus' time the Romans ruled Jerusalem and the country of Palestine. The Bible tells of several times that Jesus was in Jerusalem.

Galilee: This was the region in the north of Palestine in which Jesus grew up and spent most of his healing ministry. Almost all the disciples came from Galilee.

After Jesus healed a boy of epilepsy ■ in the Mount Hermon area, ■ he began to travel toward **Jerusalem**. As he went, he taught and preached in the towns and countryside of **Galilee**.

Sabbath/Synagogue: The Jews met in the synagogue to worship God on the Sabbath day, which is Saturday. Inside the synagogue were benches along the walls, a raised platform, oil lamps, and a cabinet to hold the Scriptures on scrolls. Men and women may have sat in separate places. "Chief seats" were reserved for elders and important visitors. Jesus once rebuked the scribes and Pharisees (see **Sabbath Laws** on page 11 and **Scribes, Pharisees** on pages 13 and 14) for taking these seats so that people could see them. The service consisted of prayer, singing psalms, reading from the Scriptures, and teaching. The man in charge, the "ruler," chose men to read and teach. Jesus was chosen to teach in synagogues many times.

Wherever Jesus went, he visited **synagogues** and was often invited to teach on the **Sabbath** day.

One Sabbath, while Jesus was teaching, a woman was there who was bent over and couldn't straighten up. She had been this way for such a long time—18 years.

Unclean Spirits, Evil Spirits, Demons, Devils, Unclean Devils: In Jesus' time people believed there were invisible beings that could get inside them, could speak for them, and could cause many kinds of diseases and disabilities. They believed these beings worked for the Devil or Satan (words that refer to that which is opposed to God). In the Bible, "unclean" means "impure."

Laws of Cleanness: These were laws the Jews believed they needed to obey in order to be "clean" or pure in the sight of God. They believed that the sick, the sinning, the dead, Gentiles (see **Gentiles** on page 44), certain animals such as swine and dogs, and people controlled by what they called unclean spirits were "unclean" or impure. They believed that if they touched or were touched by someone or something that was unclean, they became unclean, too. To be clean or pure again, the unclean had to take part in special purification rituals.

People thought the woman was being controlled by an **evil spirit.** In those days everyone believed that evil spirits were beings that could get into people and make them sick or unable to move their bodies freely. And they believed that people with evil spirits were "**unclean,**" which means "impure." People didn't want this woman to touch them, and they didn't want to touch her because they believed this would make *them* unclean, too.

When Jesus saw the woman, **he called her to come to him.** Then he said to her, "You are free!" Jesus knew that people believed an evil spirit was keeping her from being able to straighten up. But he knew that evil spirits weren't real. They were only bad thoughts that had no power over this woman—or anyone.

He knew she was free of any thought that something could make her stay bent over. God, who is the only Spirit, created her and, therefore, she was His child—always spiritual, perfect, and well. God would never allow her to be sick or in pain or bent over.

So when Jesus said to the woman, "You are free," he was telling her that she was healed before she even got to him.

Laying on of Hands/Healing by Touch: In Bible times many people believed they could be healed when they were touched by Jesus or when they touched him or his clothing.

☐ *Being touched by Jesus ("laying on of hands"):* The term, "laying on of hands," was a symbol for the power of God to heal. To Jesus, placing hands on someone didn't mean that the human hands had any real power in them to bless or to heal. Instead, it was an expression of love and compassion that helped remove the person's fear. In half of Jesus' 30 recorded healings, no mention of Jesus touching the person is made. In three of these cases, he healed people who were not even present with him. And in many of the healing stories, when Jesus touched people, the Bible records that he made it clear it was their faith that healed them.

☐ *Touching Jesus or his clothing:* Many people believed that if they touched Jesus or his clothing they would be healed. Jesus was so spiritually minded that he was able to know people's need for healing. Those who reached out were healed because of Jesus' clear understanding of the all-power of God, who is Spirit, to heal.

Jesus then reached out and **touched** the woman. This must have made her feel so loved and cared for. She was no longer afraid—and she was healed immediately. She was able to stand up straight!

Think how grateful she was to be well and strong and to be able to walk like others. People would now see her as "clean." She showed everyone how thankful she was by saying to Jesus and to the people in the synagogue how great and powerful God was. She was certainly brave to speak out!

But someone there was very angry about this wonderful healing.

This was the ruler of the synagogue. He was angry because he believed Jesus had broken the Fourth Commandment, which says the Sabbath should be kept holy. He, like most Jews, believed that people should rest on the Sabbath day.

The Jewish leaders had **laws** listing what kind of work was allowed and what kind was not allowed on the Sabbath. They said that healing was work that was *not* allowed unless the sickness was very bad. The ruler was thinking that Jesus should have waited until the Sabbath was over to heal this woman.

The ruler told everyone, "There are six days when people can work. Come and be healed on *those* days— but not on the Sabbath."

Where the Spirit of the Lord is, there is liberty.

II Corinthians 3:17

God, who is Spirit, is infinite. That means God's goodness, perfection, love, and harmony are everywhere. When we are sick, in pain, or afraid, we can turn our thoughts to this great truth and know that God gives us good only. Then we'll feel the presence and power of God, Spirit, and be free of anything God doesn't give us!

Here Jesus also said that "Satan" had bound this woman. This term is used in the Bible to mean "evil"—that which is the opposite of God. Jesus once said about Satan or the Devil that "there is no truth in him" and that "he is a liar, and the father of it" (John 8:44). Jesus knew that God is everywhere and all powerful and that this truth freed the woman from believing in any other power.

WHAT CAN YOU DO?

Standing up for what is right may seem hard to do sometimes. Especially when everyone around you doesn't agree with you. But you can know, as Jesus did when he stood up to the ruler, that your Father-Mother God loves you. God gives you the right words to say and keeps you safe from any harm. You can be strong and unafraid, knowing that God is always right there with you.

Jesus knew that it was right to heal every day. He knew that obeying the Jewish leaders' Sabbath law kept people from loving and helping others—work that God certainly approves. What he said next may have helped everyone see that the ruler and those who agreed with him were pretending. They were *acting* like they loved people more than animals, but they *really* cared more for their animals. He said, "All of you are pretenders. Doesn't each of you on the Sabbath day untie your ox or your donkey and set it free from the barn so you can lead it to water? Then shouldn't this **daughter of Abraham,** who hasn't been able to straighten up for 18 years, be set free—be healed—on the Sabbath day?"

What Jesus said made the ruler and those who agreed with him look silly. Everyone else now understood that what the ruler had said wasn't right at all. And they were so happy about all of Jesus' wonderful healings.

Man Healed of Swelling

Luke 14:1-6

Jerusalem: See page 6.

Pharisees: The Pharisees were a group of men who loved to obey the Ten Commandments. But they also obeyed hundreds of other laws made by Jews through the years. Many Jews looked up to the Pharisees. So the Pharisees began to feel that they were more obedient to God's commands than other people were. And they felt they needed to watch everyone else to make sure they were obeying all the laws. The laws became so important to the Pharisees that they began to forget the real meaning, the spirit, of the Commandments, which was love for God and for others. Jesus, on the other hand, loved the true meaning of the Commandments. He taught people about God's love, and he proved this love by healing. If a Jewish law kept him from loving and healing, Jesus didn't obey it. This upset the Pharisees. It also bothered them that big crowds of people were following Jesus and not them.

After Jesus healed a woman whose back was bent, he continued traveling through cities and villages on his way to **Jerusalem**.

In one of these cities, Jesus was invited to have dinner in the house of a leader of the **Pharisees.** The leader and his guests were all watching Jesus to see what he would do or say. And they thought they had a good reason to watch him.

Sabbath/Synagogue: See page 7.

Scribes: These were men who copied the Jewish law (the "Torah"—the first five books of the Bible—which includes the Commandments) onto scrolls from other scrolls. They studied the Torah as well as many unwritten laws. Some scribes taught the meaning of all these laws and how people should obey them. But the scribes simply quoted words. Their teaching lacked the authority of Jesus' teaching. Jesus taught with absolute, unquestioned confidence in God's all-power. And this teaching resulted in healing.

See the following stories:
☐ "Man Healed of Mental Illness (Capernaum)," *Jesus' Healings, Part 1*, page 6.
☐ "Peter's Mother-in-Law Healed of Fever," *Jesus' Healings, Part 1*, page 12.
☐ "Man with Withered Hand Healed," *Jesus' Healings, Part 1*, page 29.
☐ "Man Healed of Disability," *Jesus' Healings, Part 2*, page 36.
☐ "Woman Healed of Back Problem," *Jesus' Healings, Part 3*, page 6.

This Commandment can be found in Exodus 20:8.

Sabbath Laws: See page 11.

It was the **Sabbath** day. The Pharisee's guests were other Pharisees as well as **scribes,** who were also called lawyers. Perhaps they had heard that Jesus healed people on the Sabbath day. ■ They believed that when he did this he broke the Fourth Commandment— "Remember the Sabbath day, to keep it holy." ■ But Jesus knew that by doing good works through God's power, he was keeping the Sabbath holy.

The Jewish leaders made **Sabbath laws** that listed the kind of work that was allowed on this day and the kind that was not. They believed healing was work and *not* allowed unless the sickness was so bad that it couldn't wait until after the Sabbath.

Perhaps the Pharisees and scribes were watching to see what Jesus would do because they wanted to accuse him of breaking a Sabbath law. They may have thought they could get rid of him so the people would follow *them*, instead of Jesus. They didn't have to wait long to see what would happen, because right in front of Jesus was a man who needed to be healed.

This man had a sickness that made his body swollen. ■

Jesus surprised the Pharisees and scribes by asking them the very thing that they were thinking about. He said, "Does the law allow healing on the Sabbath day?" The Pharisees just sat there and didn't answer Jesus.

Next, Jesus reached out and **touched the man** who was sick. The man must have felt so loved by Jesus. Jesus was always praying, always filling his thought with love and truth from God. He knew that God created this man—and all of His children—spiritual and healthy, so there was just no place for sickness. He knew the truth that God always loves His children and does not allow anything bad to happen to them.

The truth Jesus knew was his prayer. And this prayer healed the man instantly! Think how happy he was to be free of this sickness!

Luke says the man had "dropsy" (Luke 14:2). This word is used in the Bible to mean a condition in which a person's body or some part of it was swollen.

Laying on of Hands/Healing by Touch: See page 10.

Be strong and of a good courage, fear not, nor be afraid of them: for the Lord thy God, he it is that doth go with thee; he will not fail thee, nor forsake thee.

Deuteronomy 31:6

Jesus knew that God was always with him, always showing him the best thing to say or do. So when others were unkind or angry with him, Jesus wasn't afraid. Because he always did what God told him to do, he knew that God, who is all-powerful, was right there with him, keeping him safe. Jesus' example helps us see that God is with us always, too. So if we are sick or someone is angry with us, we can be unafraid and know God is in control.

Here the King James Version uses the word "ass," meaning "donkey." However, many early manuscripts say "son" (Luke 14:5).

The Jewish laws allowed certain types of work to be done on the Sabbath. One of these was to pull a child or an animal out of a hole dug in the ground (like a pit or a well). But these laws did not allow healing on the Sabbath unless the person was expected to die.

?

WHAT CAN YOU DO?

When you know it's right to do something, you can be brave and do it. Just as Jesus had to stand up to the Jewish leaders who were angry with him, you can stand up to anyone who tries to stop you from doing good. God is loving you every minute, and He gives you the strength to do whatever you need to do.

After Jesus healed the man, he sent him on his way. Perhaps he did this so the man wouldn't have to answer questions from the Pharisees and scribes about being healed on the Sabbath.

But Jesus loved everyone, even the Pharisees. He turned to them and asked them another question, "If your son or your ox fell into a well on the Sabbath, wouldn't you pull him out right away?" ■ Jesus knew that all of them would help their children or animals.

But the Pharisees didn't answer him. They couldn't answer because if they admitted that they would pull their child or ox out on the Sabbath, they would have to admit that healing this man was the right and loving thing to do on the Sabbath. There wasn't anything they could say. They knew that Jesus was right. Loving and healing is always right!

Ten Men Healed of Leprosy

Luke 17:11-19

Galilee: See page 6.

Jerusalem: See page 6.

Samaria: This was the region between Galilee and Judea. The Samaritans and the Jews had many long-standing religious disagreements. The Jews saw the Samaritans as a mixed race, as foreigners. The Samaritans accepted only the first five books of the Bible (the books called the Torah, or Law), and they differed from the Jews in their interpretation of the laws. They also didn't agree that the Temple should be built in Jerusalem and, instead, built one at Mt. Gerizim.

Leprosy: In the Bible the word "leprosy" can mean a variety of skin diseases. If people had a skin disease, they had to go to one of the Jewish priests, who would tell them what kind of skin disease it was. If it was serious, the priest called it "leprosy." The priests were important religious leaders. They proudly took turns working at the Temple in Jerusalem. On certain occasions they said special prayers or blessings, blew large trumpets, and blew the shofar (a trumpet made from a ram's horn). They performed many rituals that the Jews believed would make people "clean" or pure. (See **Purification Rituals** on page 19.)

As Jesus was traveling from **Galilee** to **Jerusalem**, he stopped along the way to teach and to heal. In one of the places he stopped, he healed a woman whose back was bent, and in another place he healed a man whose body was very swollen.

On this day, he was going through the land of **Samaria.** Usually, Jews didn't travel in Samaria because Jews and Samaritans didn't get along with each other. But Jesus loved everyone. He knew they were all the children of God who is the Father and Mother of everyone.

When he was going into a town, 10 lepers outside the city gate were coming toward him. They were called "lepers" because they had **leprosy**, a kind of sickness that made their skin look ugly.

Laws of Cleanness: See page 8.

Laws of Cleanness—Leprosy: Those judged by a priest to have leprosy were called "lepers" and were said to be "unclean," meaning "impure." The priest told them to obey the laws regarding uncleanness. Lepers had to live outside the town, away from anyone except other lepers. They were not allowed to go to the Temple in Jerusalem. The law said that if people touched or were touched by a leper, they would also become unclean, or impure. Once a leper was healed, he had to go back to the priest to be declared "clean."

Teacher/Master: The Hebrew and Greek words that mean "teacher" or "master" were titles of respect. People called Jesus by these titles not because he had gone to a special school. It was because he spoke with great power and understanding when he taught about God and His laws.

See "Man Healed of Leprosy," *Jesus' Healings, Part 1*, page 16.

Jewish laws said that anyone with leprosy had to stay away from other people. The laws also said that lepers were supposed to call out, "**Unclean! Unclean!**" to warn people to stay away from them. But when the lepers saw Jesus, they shouted something else instead.

They called out, "Jesus, **Master,** have mercy on us!"

Perhaps they had heard about Jesus and knew how kind he was and that he had healed people, including another leper. ■ They were asking Jesus to show love and tenderness by healing them. How they longed for kindness!

Did Jesus turn away from these people who needed help?

Be ye therefore perfect, even as your Father which is in heaven is perfect.

Matthew 5:48

How wonderful it is to know what is really true about God and His children! God created every one of us in His image and likeness. That means we are all His spiritual reflections—perfect, just as He is perfect. Jesus knew that since God's children are perfect, sickness is never a part of them. They always reflect God and are healthy. This powerful truth healed people instantly. We can know the truth and heal just as Jesus did.

Of course he didn't turn away. He was always ready to answer a call for help. Jesus was always praying—knowing that God, good, is the only power. When he saw the 10 lepers, he wasn't bothered by how their skin looked. He didn't even think of them as lepers. He saw them as God's children, created in God's image and likeness, healthy, pure, loved, and always cared for by God.

Jesus said to the men, "**Go and show yourselves to the priests.**" This was like saying the lepers were already healed because lepers wouldn't go to a priest unless they thought they were healed. The Jewish law said that a priest had to look at the lepers' skin carefully. If the priest said the men were healed, they could then go back home and live like everyone else.

WHAT CAN YOU DO?

Being grateful for all the ways (both little and big) that God loves and takes care of you is such a good thing to do. When your thoughts are filled with God's goodness, there's just no room for bad thoughts. Giving thanks to God makes you happy and healthy. Each day you can find wonderful ways that God loves you and every one of His children. Just count all the ways. Your thanksgiving will bless you and the whole world.

Happy gratitude days!

Right away, they all obeyed Jesus and started off to see the priests. If Jesus healed others, they had faith that he would heal them, too.

And he did. As the men were walking away, they were all healed. They must have been so happy about this amazing thing that had happened to them! Perhaps they thought about how their lives would change and how they could be back with their families and friends again.

But one of the men stopped. When he saw that he was healed, he turned back. And in a very loud voice he shouted how good God was and how thankful he was to be healed.

Then, he came back and threw himself on the ground in front of Jesus, and thanked him. What was surprising was that the man wasn't even a Jew. He was a Samaritan. And a Samaritan never got close to a Jew.

Jesus said, "Weren't there 10 men healed? Why is this Samaritan the only one who turned back to give thanks to God?" Jesus knew that giving thanks helps people feel God's love. It also helps them remember His goodness long after they're healed.

He then told the man, "Get up and go on your way! **Your faith has made you completely well.**" Jesus knew that trust in God was important in healing, and he wanted the man to know it. Think what this must have meant to this man to learn that faith in God brought this wonderful healing!

Healing by Faith: In thirteen of Jesus' healings, "faith" or "believing" is mentioned as important in the healing process. The Greek word for "faith," means "conviction" or "belief." To have conviction means "to be firm." Jesus told his disciples to "have faith in God" and went on to tell them about the importance of not doubting (Mark 11:22, 23). When he asked people to have faith or to believe, Jesus wanted them to be firm in their understanding that he healed by the power of God. In Mark he said that everyone who believed could heal through this power (Mark 16:17, 18). Many people who were healed by Jesus had faith in him as the "Messiah" or "Christ." They sometimes called him the "Son of David" or "Son of God," which are terms that mean "Messiah" or "Christ" (see **Messiah/Christ,** p. 5.) These terms came to stand for Jesus' spiritual nature—the influence of God, Spirit, in thought. This Christ-nature healed because it was the power of God. Jesus was constantly knowing that he was at one with God, that he was God's beloved Son. He knew God's power healed, and he proved it over and over again. He deserved to be called "Christ" Jesus because of his complete trust in God. When people who were healed said they believed in Christ Jesus, they were saying that they understood Jesus healed through the power of God. By having faith in Christ Jesus and his teachings and healings, people were affirming the power of God in their own lives. This faith helped people see that they, too, could overcome sickness, sin, and death by following Christ Jesus' example.

Woman Healed of Adultery

John 8:1-11

Jerusalem: See page 6.

Temple: See page 26.

Messiah/Christ: See page 5.

Scribes: See page 14.

Pharisees: See page 13.

Mount of Olives: From this large hill on the east side of Jerusalem, every road to the city was visible. When people like Jesus visited Jerusalem and couldn't find a place to spend the night in the city, they stayed on the Mount. Olive trees grew abundantly there. One area of the Mount was called Gethsemane (the Hebrew word for "oil press") and was a garden area where olives were processed to make olive oil. Jesus often prayed there (see Matthew 26:36-46; Mark 14:32-42; Luke 22:39-46).

Jesus traveled to **Jerusalem** and went to the **Temple.** There, people crowded around him to hear him teach. Some thought he was the **Messiah**—a special king they believed God would send to help and heal them.

The **scribes** and **Pharisees** in Jerusalem weren't happy because the people were listening to Jesus instead of to them. They argued with Jesus and even tried to have him arrested. In the evening, Jesus went to the **Mount of Olives** to spend the night. This was a high hill across a valley from Jerusalem that was covered with olive trees. Jesus was probably praying most of the night, feeling God's goodness and power right there with him.

As soon as the sun came up, he was back in the Temple teaching again.

Suddenly, some scribes and Pharisees pushed through the crowd of people who were listening to Jesus. They had a woman with them, and they made her stand right in front of Jesus. "**Master,**" they said to him, "this woman was caught committing adultery. **The law of Moses** says that people who do this should be stoned. What do you say?"

The scribes and Pharisees were trying to trick Jesus. If he said they *shouldn't* stone her, they would say he was disobeying Moses and the Jewish law. But if he said they *should* stone her, he would be going against what he taught about God as merciful. It seemed that no matter what answer he gave, he would look bad, and the people might not listen to him any more.

Instead of answering the scribes and Pharisees, Jesus stooped down and wrote with his finger on the ground. He must have been praying—listening to God's angel messages that would tell him just what to say.

Teacher/Master: See page 18.

Law about Adultery: The Seventh Commandment is "Thou shalt not commit adultery" (Exodus 20:14). People commit adultery if they break their wedding promise and make love to someone they are not married to. The law stated that the punishment for both the man and the woman was death by stoning. But in Jesus' time, the law was not being completely obeyed.

If the scribes and Pharisees had obeyed the law, they also would have brought the *man* who committed adultery, as he deserved the same punishment. In addition, they would have brought two witnesses to prove guilt. And the guilty man and woman would have been taken to the proper authorities, not to a teacher like Jesus.

The King James Version includes the words "as though he heard them not" (John 8:6). This phrase was added by the translators. Here are two other possible reasons for Jesus' stooping down:
☐ Perhaps he was thinking about his answer quietly, refusing to let their tricks bother him.
☐ By turning away from the scribes and Pharisees, he may have been showing that his purpose was not to judge or punish others but to teach about God's deeper law of love, mercy, and healing.

WHAT CAN YOU DO?

If you are ever in a place where people are angry at you for no reason, will you be angry back? If they are trying to get you into trouble, will you be upset? Jesus knew that wherever he was and whatever was going on around him, God, his Father, was always right there with him. You can know that, too. Like Jesus, you can calmly turn your thought away from the angry faces. And when your thought is quiet, you'll hear the right ideas from God—just as Jesus did. God's ideas tell you exactly what to say or do to help everyone calm down.

When the men kept asking him questions, Jesus stood up and said, "If there is a man here who has never sinned—has never done anything wrong—let him be the first to throw a stone at her." Then he bent down and wrote again on the ground.

When the scribes and Pharisees heard that, they must have thought about their own lives. The first one to admit to himself that he had done things that were wrong was the oldest man. He knew he couldn't throw the first stone. Without saying a word, he walked away. And one by one all the rest did the same.

These men had tried to trick Jesus and make him look bad. Instead, they were the ones that looked bad. At last, Jesus was left alone, with the woman still standing where they left her.

Sir/Lord: These terms are titles of respect and refer to a person of authority.

Jesus' Treatment of Women: See page 9.

Judge not according to the appearance, but judge righteous judgment.

John 7:24

Jesus knew that the right way to judge people is by how God sees them. The woman who was brought to him appeared to be a sinner, but Jesus judged the right way. He knew that God, who is Spirit, created this woman in His image and likeness and, therefore, she was His spiritual, perfect creation. He knew that God kept her that way—always. Because Jesus judged rightly, the woman was healed. When we judge rightly and see others as God sees them, this is a powerful prayer that results in healing. What happiness we bring to those around us when we judge rightly!

Jesus stood up, and seeing no one but the woman, said to her, "Where are the men who brought you here? Isn't anyone left to call you a sinner and try to punish you?"

"No one, **Sir,**" she replied.

"Neither do I call you a sinner," answered Jesus. Jesus didn't call her a sinner because he didn't think of her that way. He knew that God created everyone pure and good, and this is always the truth.

Then Jesus said good-bye with these words: "Go, and don't sin anymore."

Think how grateful this woman must have been to Jesus. **The kindness and love he had shown her** that day must have helped her understand that she was God's child and would be able to do good from that time on.

Man Healed of Blindness from Birth

John 9:1-7

Temple: The Temple in Jerusalem (see **Jerusalem,** page 6) was the center of the Jews' religious worship. More than just a place of prayer and public worship, the Temple symbolized the presence of God. It was planned by King David almost 1,000 years before Jesus and was built by his son Solomon, when he became king. It was very large and beautiful and built by skilled workers using the finest wood, stone, silver, and gold. The Temple contained a room called the "Holy of Holies," where the ark was kept. The ark was a chest that contained Moses' Ten Commandments on stone tablets, as well as other articles. The ark had disappeared by Jesus' time. The Temple was destroyed by an enemy in 586 B.C. and then rebuilt and finished in 515 B.C. King Herod the Great began to expand and rebuild the Temple in 20 B.C. It was finished in 64 A.D. Jesus' parents took him to the Temple for a special ritual when he was a baby. And when he was 12 years old, he and his parents traveled from Nazareth to the Temple for a festival. Jesus stayed to listen to and question the teachers there. When Jesus grew up, he traveled to Jerusalem for festivals and sometimes taught in the Temple area. Once or twice Jesus made people leave this area when they did not treat it with respect.

Messiah/Christ: See page 5.

Jesus had been in the **Temple** in **Jerusalem.** There, he taught many people and healed a woman of sin. He also argued with the Jewish leaders. He told them God was his Father and that he was "sent" from God. He meant that he was the **Messiah** or **Christ** that God had sent to help everyone see the power of God's love in their lives.

When he told them he was sent from God, they didn't believe him and were so angry that they picked up stones to kill him. But he slipped away from them.

Jesus and his disciples had come to Jerusalem for the **Feast of Tabernacles.** The streets were filled with people. Many beggars had come to ask for money. As he was walking in the city with his **disciples,** Jesus saw one of these beggars. This man had been born blind. The disciples saw him, too. They turned to Jesus and asked him, "**Master,** why was this man born blind? Who sinned—who did wrong—to make him blind? The man or his parents?"

Most people believed that it was possible to sin before birth. They also thought that if parents sinned, something bad could happen to their children. But Jesus didn't believe this. He told his disciples, "This blindness wasn't caused by sin—either this man's sin or his parents' sin." Jesus knew that God, who is good, creates everyone in His image and likeness. His creation is good and cannot sin. Jesus said, "We're going to see God's work—God's true creation—here."

Feast of Tabernacles: This was one of three great festivals held in Jerusalem. People built simple shelters out of branches and vines and slept and ate there during the festival. It reminded them of when the Jews wandered in the wilderness for 40 years, living in tents. Water and light were two important symbols used at the festival and in this healing story.

The priests participated in the ritual of gathering water from the Pool of Siloam each day and bringing it to the Temple altar for a gratitude offering. At night, the Temple (see **Temple,** page 26) area was lighted with huge Menorahs (oil lamp stands).

Disciples: The Greek word for "disciple" means "learner," or "student." In the New Testament, this word often refers to Jesus' 12 disciples. But it could mean anyone—man, woman, or child— who is a student and follower of the ideas of a teacher.

Teacher/Master: See page 18.

Light of the World: Jesus said
that he was sent by God to be the
"light of the world." This light was
the truth Jesus knew and lived. He
always saw clearly just what was
true about everyone. He knew
that God was all good and all
powerful and that He made
everyone in His image and
likeness, perfect and good, too.
The truth he knew was like a light
that destroyed the darkness of
sickness, sin, and death.

*The entrance of thy
words giveth light; it
giveth understanding
unto the simple.*

Psalm 119:130

Feeling God's goodness and love is so
wonderful. It happens when we open
our thought to good and close it to the
bad. When God's good ideas are all
that we have in our thought, it's like a
room filled with light. No darkness can
enter. The light fills all the space, and
the darkness has no power or place to
be. So no dark thoughts about sickness
or hurt or sadness or death can have a
place in our thinking when it is filled
with God's good thoughts. Jesus knew
that everyone can understand that they
are loved and protected by God. When
we keep our thought filled with God's
good ideas, this brings healing to us—
and to our friends and family, too.

Then he told his disciples, "During the day we must
do the works of God who sent me. ■ At night you
won't be able to work." Perhaps Jesus was telling his
disciples that they must learn to heal by understanding
God's true spiritual creation while he was there to
teach them (day). When he was gone (night), they
wouldn't have him there to show them how to do it.
Jesus continued, "I am the **light of the world.**" Jesus'
light was the truth that he knew about God's power
and love, which was always with everyone.

Next, Jesus did something so the man would know he
was going to be healed.

Here, the Bible says that Jesus **spit** (See **Spit** below) on the dusty ground, made some clay, and spread it on the eyes of the blind man.

Spit: In Jesus' times spit had at least two symbolic meanings:

☐ *Healing*—People thought of spit as a remedy for small wounds. So spit became a symbol for healing. Perhaps Jesus used spit in his healings to help people understand that he was going to heal them. Jesus knew that spit had no power to heal. And no one would have thought that touching parts of the face with spit could heal deafness, speech problems, or blindness. (See **Laying on of Hands/Healing by Touch** below.)

☐ *Disapproval*—Spitting also showed that something was worthless. When he used spit in his healings, Jesus might have been showing that the disability— deafness, speech problem, or blindness—was powerless. Jesus always knew that God made everyone in His image and likeness and kept them that way. So spitting could show that he was rejecting the thought that anyone could be disabled in any way—when God is all-powerful and good.

Laying on of Hands/Healing by Touch: See page 10.

Jesus made some clay ▪ and spread it on the man's eyes. The man had heard Jesus talking to his disciples about how important it was to do God's work. He may have thought, as many people did, that clay was a symbol of healing. And he must have felt Jesus' kindness and love in his gentle **touch.** This may have helped the man understand that Jesus knew the power of God was right there to heal him.

Jesus knew that the clay had no power to heal. It was the thoughts from God that had power. And these thoughts were not about this man being blind. They were about his being God's perfect child, made in God's image, spiritual, and able to see perfectly.

But what would Jesus do next?

Pool of Siloam: Jerusalem was built on the top of a hill so the people would be safe. But the city had no water. An enemy could keep the people in the city locked behind the city walls until they got so thirsty, they would give up. So in 715 B.C., King Hezekiah built a tunnel that carried water from a spring outside the city wall into a pool he had dug inside the city. The pool was called "Siloam" which meant "sent" because fresh water was now secretly sent from outside.

WHAT CAN YOU DO?

Many people believe that sickness, disabilities, or personality faults are inherited. Jesus didn't believe that the man's blindness came from his parents or from anything the man did wrong. You can know, just like Jesus, that the only real parent anyone has is God.

Your Father-Mother God gives only good—gives you everything you need to be healthy, strong, smart, loving, and peaceful. You can know this, too, about your parents and your brothers and sisters. You will find that the truth you know about yourself and others is a prayer that heals.

He said to the man, "Go and wash in the **Pool of Siloam.**" This was a large pool of water in the city. The name, "Siloam," meant "sent." When the man heard Jesus say he was *sent* from God, he may have asked himself if Jesus was a prophet who could heal. Then when Jesus told him to go to the Pool of Siloam, which everyone knew also meant *sent*, this must have answered his question. It must have helped him have faith in the power of God to heal him.

The man went to the pool, washed off the clay, and returned—seeing. For the first time in his life! Imagine how amazed and grateful he must have been! He could see his family and friends now. And he could also see with his heart that he and his parents were sinless children of God.

That day the disciples learned not to look for what caused a sickness or disability but to see God's good and true creation always. This would help them do God's work and become better healers.

Lazarus Brought Back to Life

John 11:1-45

Jerusalem: See page 6.

Disciples: See page 27.

Judea: This is the region in the south of Palestine. Jerusalem, where many of Jesus' healings occurred, and Bethlehem, where he was born, are in Judea.

Jordan River: In the Bible the Jordan is an important river and is mentioned often. Elisha directed Naaman to wash in the Jordan to be healed of leprosy. John the Baptist preached by the Jordan and baptized Jesus there. The Jordan river flows from the mountains in the north into a lake called the Sea of Galilee, then down through the Jordan Valley until it reaches the Dead Sea, the lowest spot on earth—1,300 feet below sea level.

Perea: Perea was the land to the east of the Jordan River where John the Baptist preached. When traveling north and south, many Jews went through Perea to avoid Samaria on the west side of the river (see **Samaria,** page 17).

When Jesus healed the man in **Jerusalem** who was blind from birth, many Jewish leaders argued with him. They refused to believe he healed through the power of God. Some even tried to kill him.

But Jesus and his **disciples** escaped from Jerusalem, which was in **Judea,** and crossed the **Jordan River** to **Perea.** The people there came and listened to him. Many believed he was sent from God, and that his power to heal was from God.

In John 11:2 the Bible tells us that Mary anointed Jesus' feet at a dinner where Jesus was the honored guest. This dinner occurred after Jesus restored Lazarus to life. Mary spread precious perfume on Jesus' feet and wiped them with her hair, showing her deep love, gratitude, and loyalty to Jesus (John 12:1-9). This is not the same woman who washed Jesus' feet at the home of Simon the Pharisee (Luke 7:36-50).

Sir/Lord: See page 25.

Son of Man/Son of God:
Jesus called himself both the "Son of man" and the "Son of God." When he called himself the Son of man, he was referring to himself as a human being like any other person. When he called himself the Son of God, he was referring to his spiritual nature. Although Jesus knew that all people are children of God, he understood and demonstrated his sonship more perfectly than all others. By using both of these terms for himself when he healed, perhaps Jesus wanted people to see that although he was human, it was his spirituality that enabled him to heal. This may have helped people understand that their own power to heal was a result of their spiritual nature as sons and daughters of God, with absolute faith in God's love and all-power. Jesus wanted them to know that they could heal as he did. (Other names for Son of God are "Messiah" and "Christ"—see **Messiah/Christ** on page 5.)

While Jesus was in Perea, good friends of his in Judea needed his help. They were Mary ■ and Martha and their brother Lazarus. They lived in the quiet village of Bethany, a short walk from Jerusalem. Lazarus had become very sick. Because the sisters were worried about him, they sent a message to Jesus saying, "**Lord,** the friend you love is sick." The sisters didn't ask, but they probably hoped that Jesus would come and heal their brother.

When Jesus received the news from the messenger about his friend Lazarus, he said, "This sickness is not really about death. Instead, the **Son of God** is going to show people the wonderful goodness and power of God. And because of this, the Son will be praised and honored." Jesus was speaking of himself when he used the term "Son of God."

Jesus loved Martha and her sister and Lazarus, but he didn't leave right away to help them. It may have seemed unloving, but as always, Jesus was praying to know what to do. He knew that God, who is good, created everyone and never took life away. He knew Lazarus was safe in God's love—forever. Jesus was listening for God's angel messages. He knew God would tell him just the right time to go to Bethany.

After two days, Jesus knew it was time to go. He said to his disciples, "Let's go back to Judea again." (That was where Jerusalem and Bethany were.)

But the disciples did not want to go. They said, "**Master,** the Jewish leaders tried to kill you the last time you were there. Why do you want to go back?"

Jesus reminded his disciples that he was the **light of the world.** This light was the truth about God's all-power and goodness that Jesus trusted in completely. His mission was to bring this light of truth to the world. It was God-directed, and, therefore, it would not fail. He had to complete his mission. Going to Judea was part of that. He wanted his disciples to see that because they were loyal disciples, they were part of his mission. They needed to be by his side to learn from him. There would be a time soon when he would not be with them.

Next, he said to them, "Our friend Lazarus is asleep. And I'm going to go and wake him up."

Teacher/Master: See page 18.

Light of the World: See page 28.

Here, Jesus used the Jewish concept of a day (12 hours for day and 12 for night) to discuss how he and his disciples needed to complete the mission. He encouraged his disciples to take advantage of the time he had left to be with them—and compared this time to the daylight hours in a day. At night, he would be gone, and they would have missed some important and wonderful lessons (John 11:9, 10).

Even without hearing anything more from Mary and Martha, Jesus knew that Lazarus was dead.

Jesus had brought people back to life at least twice before. But restoring them to life happened so quickly after they had died that perhaps others may have wondered if the people had really been dead. This time there would be no doubt.

Thomas: This disciple was also called "Didymus" (meaning "twin"). He doubted Jesus' resurrection without having proof (John 20:26-29).

Being buried for four days had special meaning to the Jews. They believed that people had a spirit that waited by the grave for three days hoping to return to the body. But on the fourth day, when the body began to decay, the spirit left forever. So, although raising the dead would have been surprising on *any* day, the passage of four days made this resurrection amazing.

When Jesus said that Lazarus was asleep, his disciples didn't understand. They said, "Lord, if he's asleep, he'll be all right." They probably wondered why they needed to go to that dangerous place just to wake up a friend.

But Jesus didn't mean Lazarus was asleep. This time he said to them, "Lazarus is dead. ■ And for your sakes, I'm glad I wasn't with him because now you'll really learn to trust God." He knew that what they would see there would help them understand that God is the only power. ■ Jesus said strongly, "Now let's go to him."

Thomas, one of the 12 disciples, said to the others, "Let's go to Judea and die with Jesus." Thomas thought he and the other disciples could be killed there, but he was brave and loyal to Jesus. His bravery must have helped the disciples because they decided they would go, too. They left Perea with Jesus and headed for Bethany.

As they came near the village, Jesus received the message that his friend Lazarus had been buried four days earlier. ■

Bethany was about two miles  from Jerusalem. Many Jews had come from this city to be with the sisters while they **mourned** for their brother. Some may have been people who wanted to get rid of Jesus.

The minute Martha received news that Jesus was just outside Bethany, she hurried out to meet him. But Mary stayed at the house, sitting quietly and sadly with those who came to visit her.

Martha's first words to Jesus were, "Lord, if you had been here, my brother wouldn't have died. But, I know that even now, God will give you whatever you ask."

The King James Version says Bethany was 15 furlongs from Jerusalem. A furlong is 220 yards.

Jewish Mourning Customs: In Bible times, when someone died, people visited the person's family to show their love and to help them. The usual mourning period for family members was seven days. The Jews also followed certain rituals to show their grief. Those in mourning wore clothes made of sackcloth—a rough, dark-colored material made of goat's or camel's hair. Often they "rent," or tore, their clothes. Some put ashes or dust on their heads. Immediately after a person died, the family hired "mourners" (usually women) to weep and wail—to cry out very loudly and sing sad songs. They also hired people to play musical instruments, most often flutes. The Jewish laws said that even the poorest burial must have at least two flutes and one wailing woman.

Jesus' Treatment of Women: See page 9.

Healing by Faith: See page 21.

Messiah/Christ: See page 5.

Jesus said, "Your brother will come back to life again."

Martha believed that Lazarus *would* come back to life—but not right then. She said, "I know my brother will come back to life with all good Jews in the resurrection on the "last day." "Resurrection" means "rising from the dead." Many Jews believed that all good Jews would rise from death on a special day they called the "last day."

But **Jesus wanted Martha to understand and believe** that he had the power to bring her brother back to life—right at that moment. He said to her, "I am the resurrection and the life." Jesus then told Martha that if someone believed in him—in his power over death—even if the person was dead, he or she would rise again and would understand that life is eternal. And if anyone living believed in his power, he or she would not die. He asked Martha, "Do you **believe** this?"

Martha answered him, "Yes, Lord, I do believe that you are the **Christ,** the Son of God, the one the prophets promised would come into the world." Martha may not have understood everything Jesus said, but she did believe he was the Christ, sent by God. With this new hope that her brother might be brought back to life, she hurried away to get her sister Mary. She must have wanted her to feel this same hope from the Master.

Martha called her away from the people from Jerusalem who were with her. Martha whispered, "The Master is close by and wants to see you."

Mary jumped up and hurried to Jesus. The others thought she was running to the tomb to cry about her brother's death, so they hurried after her. As a result, Mary wouldn't have much time to talk with Jesus alone. When she saw him, she fell down in front of him. Then, she said the same thing her sister had said, "Lord, if you had been here, my brother wouldn't have died."

But Jesus didn't answer her. Both Mary and the others were crying loudly. Jesus must have hoped that those he loved and taught, like Mary, would have a more spiritual thought. He wanted them to have faith that Lazarus could come back from the dead. It must have been very hard for Jesus when he saw that they still didn't trust in the power of God. ■ Jesus' only words were: "Where did you put him?"

The people said, "Come and see."

The King James Version says Jesus "groaned" (John 11:33). The Greek words here can mean he was "disturbed," "distressed," "indignant."

Some reasons Jesus may have been disturbed are:
■ His friends' limited faith and their disbelief in his mission
■ The unbelief of so many of the Jews
■ The depth of Mary's grief

The King James Version tells us that Jesus was "again groaning in himself " (John 11:38). (See sidebar on page 37.)

Laws of Cleanness—Death: The Jews believed that the dead were "unclean," or impure. Jewish laws said that anyone who touched a dead body or bier (bed) on which a dead body lay was considered unclean, or impure. The laws also said that anyone who entered the house where a dead body was laid would be unclean. Tombs were whitewashed to warn people of the uncleanness inside (Matthew 23:27). An unclean person was supposed to follow certain rituals to become clean, or pure, again.

Martha warned Jesus that by now the smell would be terrible. After four days, dead bodies begin to decay (John 11:39).

Tears came to Jesus' eyes, and he followed the people to the tomb. Some of them thought he was crying because of the death of his friend. They said, "Look, how much he loved him." Others were not so kind. They said, "If he healed the man born blind, why couldn't he keep his good friend from dying?"

Again, Jesus sighed a deep sigh. ▪ He knew that no matter what anyone said, death had no power—that life was the only power.

When Jesus got to the tomb, he stopped. A round stone covered the opening. He gave an order, "Take away the stone." Even though **the Jewish laws** said people were not supposed to get near tombs, some men rolled the great heavy stone along the groove in front of the tomb.

Earlier, Martha had told Jesus that she had faith in him. But now she was afraid again—believing that he had come too late. She told him, "He's been in there four days." ▪

Jesus reminded her, "Didn't I tell you how important it is to trust in God? Didn't I tell you that you'd see God's wonderful goodness and power?"

The crowd must have stepped back as the men rolled back the huge stone from the opening to the dark **tomb.**

But Jesus looked up and away from the tomb. He said, "Father, thank you for hearing my prayer." Jesus listened to his Father day and night and had complete faith in Him for everything. His Father loved him and guided him. Every healing was an answer to prayer.

The crowd may not have heard Jesus' prayer that day, but Jesus wanted them to know he had prayed. He said to his Father, "I know that you always hear me. But I'm speaking aloud to you so that these people standing here will believe that you sent me." No one there fully believed that Lazarus could be brought back to life.

Then with a booming voice, Jesus shouted, "Lazarus, come out!" Jesus knew Lazarus needed to wake up from believing he had ever died. He needed to see that God gave him life that could never be stopped.

In the way of righteousness is life; and in the pathway thereof there is no death.

Proverbs 12:28

Jesus always walked in the "path of righteousness." He was always praying—filling his thought with good thoughts from God. He was always knowing what was right and true— that God, Spirit, creates us. That means our life is really spiritual—and perfect. This life never ends in death. It is forever. Jesus' right knowing was powerful and resulted in people healed and restored to life. We can walk in the path of right knowing, too—just as Jesus did. And we will be able to feel the same foreverness of life that results in healing and resurrection.

39

Lazarus probably moved slowly since his arms and legs were wrapped in cloth strips that had hardened. The strips that once were wet with spices and oil were now dried stiff. And because his head was wrapped in a cloth, he couldn't see.

WHAT CAN YOU DO?

Sometimes people are sick or sad for so long that it seems like the sickness or sadness just can't be healed. If that ever happens to you, and people say it's too late to do anything about it, don't believe them. Even though it seemed too late to help Lazarus, Jesus didn't give up. He knew Lazarus was created by God and that God kept him safe forever. Jesus knew that God's love and care for all His children never ends. Jesus' great faith and understanding of God's power and love raised Lazarus from death. You can know that God, who made you and cares for you every day and night, is always telling you the truth about your life. As you listen for God's good thoughts, you'll be healed, too. It's never too late for God!

The people watched the entrance to the tomb. They were amazed when Lazarus appeared. ▨ He was still wrapped in cloth strips. And his head was wrapped in another cloth. Jesus said to the crowd, "Loose him and let him go."

Jesus had said he was going to waken Lazarus out of sleep. And that's just what he did. In fact, he woke up everyone that day—just as if they were having a bad dream. They had been dreaming that sickness and death had power, but Jesus knew the truth—that God, good, is the only power. He proved that God loves His sons and daughters and keeps them safe from sickness and death, always. He proved that life is eternal—it never ends.

What a wonderful day for Lazarus and for everyone!

Bartimaeus Healed of Blindness

Mark 10:46-52

Other accounts of this story are found in Matthew 20:29-34 and Luke 18:35-43.

The Jewish leaders were actually planning to kill Jesus.

Jerusalem: See page 6.

Disciples: See page 27.

Feast of Passover: This was an eight-day festival held in remembrance of how God saved the Jews from slavery in Egypt.

Jericho: This was a busy city down in the Jordan Valley about 15 miles northeast of Jerusalem.

Here, the Bible says Bartimaeus was the son (bar) of Timaeus (Mark 10:46). Matthew says there were two unnamed blind men (Matthew 20:30). Luke says there was one unnamed blind man (Luke 18:35).

Jesus of Nazareth: Using Jesus' hometown with his name, distinguished him from others named "Jesus."

Messiah/Christ: See page 5.

After Jesus brought his friend Lazarus back to life, the Jewish leaders began to plan how they could get rid of Jesus. ▮ So Jesus left the **Jerusalem** area and went with his **disciples** to stay in a small town several miles away. When it was almost time for the **Feast of Passover** in Jerusalem, Jesus decided to travel back to the city. On the way, he and his disciples had to pass through the city of **Jericho.** A large group of people crowded around Jesus, some following him, others lining the road to try to see him.

A blind man named Bartimaeus ▮ sat by the road begging. When he heard people talking about **Jesus of Nazareth,** Bartimaeus began to shout, "Jesus, Son of David, have mercy on me." The name "Son of David" meant "**Messiah**" or "**Christ,**" a name the Jews used for a special king or prophet they believed would come one day to help and heal them. Bartimaeus must have heard about Jesus and his healings and knew Jesus could help him.

The crowd ordered Bartimaeus to be quiet. But he wouldn't give up. In fact, he shouted even louder, "Son of David, have mercy on me."

Even with all the noise of the crowd, Jesus heard Bartimaeus and stopped. He said, "Tell that man to come here." Wherever Jesus was, he cared about people. He saw them as God saw them—as God's perfect spiritual image and likeness. And people were healed by this way of seeing.

Now, instead of trying to quiet the man, the crowd said to him, "Cheer up. He's calling you." Throwing his cloak aside, Bartimaeus jumped up and went to Jesus. He knew he would be healed.

But Jesus asked him a surprising question, "What do you want me to do for you?"

Some possible reasons the people told Bartimaeus to be quiet are:

▪ Jesus' friends didn't want people to hear Jesus called "Son of David," This meant "Messiah" and might attract the attention of the Jewish leaders, who were looking for Jesus to have him arrested.

▪ They were trying to listen to Jesus teach as they walked.

▪ They didn't want Jesus to be bothered by beggars.

Some possible reasons Bartimaeus threw his cloak aside:

▪ He wanted to get to Jesus quickly and the cloak might slow him down.

▪ As a beggar, he may have used his cloak for collecting alms (money). By casting aside the cloak, he would have been showing he was sure he could be healed and wouldn't need his beggar's cloak again.

WHAT CAN YOU DO?

If you ever have a sickness that seems hard to heal, it may be discouraging. But think about Bartimaeus. When he learned that Jesus was near, he knew he could be healed. You, too, can know that nothing is too hard to heal. Nothing is impossible to God. You're His image and likeness. Since God is perfect, you are perfect, too. And since God loves you always—He keeps you perfect. You can let God's truths be the only thing you know. Never give up on the truth—and you will be healed.

Jesus knew what Bartimaeus wanted, but he asked him to say it out loud. Bartimaeus answered, "Teacher, ▦ I want to see." Earlier Bartimaeus had called Jesus a name meaning "Messiah," which showed he believed Jesus had power from God to help him. Now, he called him "Teacher," one who taught the law of God. This showed he believed that God's law of goodness would give him his sight.

Jesus said to him, "Go on your way." ▦ Jesus was telling him he already had his sight—and to act like it. Then he said to him, "Your **faith has healed you.**" ▦ Jesus wanted him to know that he was healed through his complete trust in the power of God. Instantly, Bartimaeus understood—and he could see.

Bartimaeus was filled with joy. He could see with his eyes. And he could see—understand—the power of God's law of good. Now, he wanted to be a disciple. So he joined right in with those following Jesus ▦ up to Jerusalem. How happy everyone must have been that day!

▦

Here the Greek word translated "Lord" means "Teacher" (Mark 10:51).

Luke tells us Jesus said, "Receive thy sight" (Luke 18:42).

Healing by Faith: See page 21.

Matthew says that Jesus had compassion on two blind men. He touched their eyes, and they were healed (Matthew 20:34). (See **Laying on of Hands/Healing by Touch** on page 10.)

When Bartimaeus "followed Jesus," it probably meant that he became a disciple (Mark 10:52). Jesus had many more than 12 disciples.

Your faith should not stand in the wisdom of men, but in the power of God.

I Corinthians 2:5

Jesus had complete faith that the power of God was the only power in the world. He was able to prove God's power over and over in his daily life. We, too, can have that faith that stands with God and His power. We can have no doubt that God loves us and is able and ready to meet our every need. Right now, we can prove how powerful God is to heal and help us—just as Jesus proved it 2,000 years ago.

Zaccaeus Healed of Dishonesty

Luke 19:1-10

Jericho: See page 41.

Jerusalem: See page 6.

Feast of Passover: See page 41.

Zaccaeus: Zaccaeus was a Jew. The name "Zaccaeus" means "pure," "righteous," "innocent."

Some other reasons why Jews didn't like Zaccaeus:
He worked for the Romans who were Gentiles (see **Gentiles** below), and, therefore, was considered "unclean" (see **Laws of Cleanness** on page 8).
He worked for the Romans and, therefore, would be considered a traitor to his fellow Jews.

Gentiles: People who did not believe in the one God were called "Gentiles" by the Jews. Because Gentiles worshiped other gods, Jews considered them "unclean," or impure. So the Jews separated themselves from Gentiles to keep their religion pure. (See **Laws of Cleanness** on page 8.)

Jesus was passing through the city of **Jericho** where he had healed Bartimaeus of blindness. He was traveling to **Jerusalem** for the **Feast of Passover,** and people crowded around him to see and hear him. In the crowd was a man named **Zaccaeus.** He was the chief publican or tax collector in the area. His job was to collect tax money for the Romans. Zaccaeus was rich, and like most tax collectors, he had probably gotten rich by being dishonest. A tax collector charged higher taxes than the Romans asked for and then kept the extra money. Because of this, Jews didn't like Zaccaeus. ▪

Zaccaeus must have heard about Jesus and how he loved everybody—even tax collectors and sinners (people who did wrong things). He wanted to see this man Jesus that he had heard about. But Zaccaeus was so short that he couldn't see over the crowd. Then Zaccaeus got a bright idea!

He ran ahead and climbed up into a sycamore tree to see him! When Jesus got close to the tree, he looked up into the branches and saw Zacchaeus. Although Jesus was not from Jericho, he probably knew who he was and what people thought of him. But Jesus also knew that God who is Spirit created everyone in His image and likeness. He didn't think of Zacchaeus as a greedy, dishonest tax collector. He saw him as God's spiritual child—perfect and good.

Jesus called out to him, "Zacchaeus! Hurry! Come down! Today I must be a guest at your house." Zacchaeus must have been very surprised! He scrambled down the tree as fast as he could. And he happily welcomed Jesus into his house. But not everyone was happy about what Jesus did. The crowd began to grumble. They didn't understand why Jesus, a great teacher, had gone to the house of a sinner— someone who was "unclean," or "impure." But Jesus didn't think that way about Zacchaeus.

The Bible calls this a "sycamore" tree (Luke 19:4). However, it isn't like what is ordinarily known today as a sycamore tree. It's a type of fig tree known as a "mulberry fig." It has low, wide-spreading branches, making it easy to climb.

This was a strange thing for a very important tax collector to do. People would probably laugh at him, but Zacchaeus didn't care. He really wanted to see Jesus—and up in the tree, he could do that.

WHAT CAN YOU DO?

Do you know someone who has done bad things to you or to others? There is something you can do about it. You can listen to God! His angel thoughts will remind you that He created this person. God is our Father and our Mother. As our Mother, God loves every one of Her children. And no matter what they have done, Her children were created in Her image and likeness—pure and perfect. God always sees them this way. When you see people as God sees them, you'll begin to find the good in them. And both you and they will feel the healing power of God's goodness.

Sir/Lord: See page 25.

The Roman law said that a thief must pay back four times as much. But the Jewish law only required that a thief pay back what he stole plus one fifth, or 20 percent (Leviticus 6:1-6). Zacchaeus promised to pay back more than was required by the Jewish law.

Daughter/Son of Abraham: See page 12.

Here Jesus called himself the "Son of Man." See **Son of Man/Son of God** page 32.

See that none render evil for evil unto any man; but ever follow that which is good, both among yourselves, and to all men.

I Thessalonians 5:15

Jesus knew that even if someone is doing bad things like Zacchaeus did, it is never helpful to treat that person badly. When Jesus met Zacchaeus, he didn't see a sinner, someone who did bad things. He saw only the man God created, who is good and pure and could never do anything bad. When people we see or know are doing bad things, we can do as Jesus did. We can pray. Our prayer can be to see them as God's spiritual, perfect children. This is a prayer that brings healing and happiness to everyone.

In his prayer Jesus knew that God created Zacchaeus as His pure reflection—without sin. This prayer helped Zacchaeus see himself differently—as good and pure. He stood up straight and tall and made a promise. He said, "At this moment, **Lord,** I'm going to give half my money to poor people. And if I have cheated anyone, I will pay back that person four times what I took. ■

Jesus said to him, "Today healing has come to this family, for this man is also a **son of Abraham.**" Jesus may have meant that Zacchaeus was healed of his sin because he was like Abraham—who had faith in the one God. People would now consider Zacchaeus' house and his whole family to be "clean," or "pure." Jesus said, "My purpose in life ■ is to look for and to heal those who have lost their way." Jesus loved and cared for those who had let bad thoughts and actions make them forget God's goodness.

How happy Zacchaeus must have been to be free of the bad thoughts and actions that had kept him from feeling close to God, who is good. And what a lesson others learned that day—to see sinners in a new way—as God's children, loved and cared for by their Father.

Malchus' Ear Healed

Luke 22:47-51

Other accounts of this story are found in Matthew: 26:47-52, Mark 14:43-47, and John 18:1-11.

Jericho: See page 41.

Jerusalem: See page 6.

Disciples: See page 27.

Feast of Passover: See page 41.

Jesus would be turned over to the Romans and crucified (nailed to a cross and left until dead).

During the Feast of Passover, the Jews prepared a meal that celebrated the escape of the Jewish people from slavery in Egypt. The Passover meal Jesus ate with his disciples has since been called "The Last Supper."

Mount of Olives: See page 22.

Gethsemane: Gethsemane is the name of a garden across the eastern valley from Jerusalem on the Mount of Olives. Jesus often went there to pray. It was where his arrest took place. It had olive trees and an oil press which was used to squeeze oil from the olives. "Gethsemane" means "oil press."

After healing people in **Jericho,** Jesus continued to **Jerusalem.** Within a short time, he and the **disciples** arrived for the **Feast of Passover.** During Passover week, Jesus told his disciples that he would be crucified. ■ He arranged to be with them for one last supper—the Passover meal. ■ During this meal, Jesus told his disciples that one of them would betray him, which meant turn him over to the Jewish leaders. These leaders wanted to arrest him and have him killed.

After the meal, he left the city with 11 of the disciples to go to the **Mount of Olives.** There, among the olive trees in a place called **Gethsemane,** Jesus asked his disciples to pray. He then went a little distance away to pray by himself. When he returned to the disciples, he found them sleeping.

Jesus began to tell them it was important for them to pray. While he was speaking, they heard people coming up the hill toward them.

The gospels tell us who the people were who came to arrest Jesus: chief priests, elders, scribes, captains of the Temple, men and officers from the chief priests, and Pharisees. Both Jews and Romans were among the crowd.

The gospels also say that these men came with swords and clubs, lanterns and torches (Matt 26:47; Mark 14:43; Luke 22:52; John 18:3).

John says that when Jesus saw Judas and the band of men coming closer, he stepped forward to meet them and asked them who they were looking for. They replied, "Jesus of Nazareth." He then told them, "I am he." The Greek words here are actually "I am," without the word "he." "I Am" is a name for God. By saying God's name, Jesus may have been stating that God's power was present at that moment and there was no other power. The soldiers felt the power of Jesus' thought. They immediately fell on the ground (John 18:4-6). Jesus knew that the soldiers were powerless to do anything to him unless he allowed it.

Matthew and Mark say Judas actually kissed Jesus, saying "Hail, Master," or "Master, Master." (Matthew 26:49; Mark 14:45).

Here Jesus calls himself the "Son of man." See **Son of Man/Son of God** on page 32.

As the people ■ came closer, Jesus and the disciples could see that the group was large. And leading them was Judas, one of Jesus' 12 disciples. ▨

Judas walked right up to Jesus and was ready to kiss him on the cheek. This is how friends said "hello" to each other in that country. But Jesus stopped Judas ▪ with these words, "Are you going to point me out to the enemy with a kiss?" ▨

How hard this must have been for Jesus and for the 11 disciples! Judas had been their friend, traveling with them, learning from Jesus, and even being sent out with them to heal. And now Judas had betrayed Jesus and was bringing soldiers to arrest him.

The frightened disciples asked Jesus, "**Lord,** shall we fight them with our swords?"

Suddenly, Peter took out a sword, struck Malchus, a servant of the **high priest,** and cut off his ear. Instantly Jesus said, "Enough of this. Let them have their way." He was telling the disciples that this was not the way to fight back. Jesus always met hatred with love. He did not let anger and fear control him.

Judas may have betrayed Jesus for any of the following reasons:
☐ He wanted the money and popularity. (The Jewish leaders paid him 30 pieces of silver.)
☐ He wanted to force Jesus to use his powers to become king.
☐ He saw Jesus' mission as a lost cause and felt it was time to think of his own safety.

Sir/Lord: See page 25.

John tells us the names of the disciple and the servant (John 18: 10).

High Priest: This person was the head priest at the Temple. See **Temple** on page 26.

Not my will, but thine, be done.

Luke 22:42

To Jesus, praying was like breathing: he never stopped doing it. He was always feeling God's presence caring for him, loving him, showing him what to do and what to say. Jesus knew that God is Love and is the only power in the universe. Therefore God's will always blesses everyone. When something in his life looked hard to face, Jesus prayed to let go of the way *he* thought things should work out and to trust *God's* will. When something in *our* life seems hard, we can trust God, too. We'll find that everyone involved is blessed when we do that. Each day we can turn to God with the prayer that Jesus prayed in Gethsemane: "Not my will, but thine, be done."

Laying on of Hands/Healing by Touch: See page 10.

This last experience with their Master showed the disciples how they must stand up to the hatred that they would have to endure after he left them. They were not to fight back with the world's weapons but were to stand up to it with God's love for others.

WHAT CAN YOU DO?

Sometimes someone may act like an enemy and try to hurt you—by hitting or punching, or hurting your feelings or trying to get you in trouble. And you may think the best thing to do is to hurt back. Jesus showed his disciples what to do when someone acted that way. When enemies came to arrest Jesus and harm him, he was ready with thoughts of love that were powerful and healing. Instead of getting angry, Jesus stayed calm. Instead of hating, Jesus showed love. Instead of hurting back, Jesus healed. As we listen to God's messages, we'll find ways to be calm, show love, and heal, too.

And at that moment, with soldiers all around to arrest him, Jesus reached out with love and **touched** Malchus' ear. And he was healed—right then! Jesus' life was a life of constant prayer. So he was always ready and willing to help and heal anyone, anywhere, any time— even if it was an enemy, like Malchus. He knew the truth about them—that they were God's children— spiritual and perfect.

Right in the midst of hatred and fear, Jesus showed the healing power of God's love. What a lesson for everyone! ■

Jesus' Resurrection

John 20:1-18

Other accounts of this story are found in Matthew: 28:1-10, Mark 16:1-8, and Luke 24:1-12.

The Jewish leaders turned Jesus over to the Romans, falsely accusing him of stirring up the people and wanting to be king. Pilate, the Roman governor, ordered Jesus to be crucified (nailed to a cross and left until dead) at the insistence of the Jewish leaders (Matthew 27:35; Mark 15:25; Luke 23:33; John 19:18).

Joseph of Arimathea: This man was a member of the Sanhedrin, the council of Jewish leaders in Jerusalem.

Jewish Burial Customs: See page 39.

Nicodemus: This man was a synagogue ruler, a teacher of the Jews, and also a member of the Sanhedrin. Once, he met with Jesus in secret—after dark—to talk with him (John 3:1-8).

The word "tomb" is often referred to as "sepulchre" in the Bible.

Sabbath Laws: See page 11.

Jesus had been crucified. **Joseph of Arimathea,** who was secretly a disciple of Jesus, asked Pilate, the Roman governor, to let him take Jesus' body and **bury** it. Pilate gave him permission.

Another secret disciple, **Nicodemus,** came with expensive spices. He helped Joseph prepare the body for burial. The two wrapped it in linen cloths and used the spices to perfume it. After this, the two men placed the body in a tomb that had not been used before. The tomb was carved out of a cave that was in a garden. A heavy, round tomb stone was rolled in front of the entrance to the tomb to seal it.

The crucifixion occurred on Friday. The two men had to prepare the body for burial very quickly because the Sabbath began at sundown. **Jewish law** did not allow any work to be done on the Sabbath.

On Sunday morning, while it was still dark, **Mary Magdalene** went to the tomb. ■ This woman was a friend and disciple of Jesus.

What she saw when she got to the tomb was amazing to her! The heavy tomb stone had been rolled away from the entrance. When Mary saw this, she thought someone had taken Jesus' body.

She wanted to tell someone about it right away.

She ran quickly and found two of Jesus' **disciples**— Peter  and John.  She was probably breathless from running when she said to them, "They took the **Lord** from the tomb, and we  don't know where they have put him."

Disciples: See page 27.

Peter was considered to be eager, quick and enthusiastic. He became a leader in the early Christian church.

The book of John never names this disciple but refers to him as the "other disciple, whom Jesus loved" (John 20:2). No one knows for sure who this disciple is. Traditionally, he has been thought to be John, who was probably the youngest of the 12. He was known for his love for others as well as Jesus' love for him. (See Disciples on page 27.)

Sir/Lord: See page 25.

While John doesn't mention the other women, Mary's remark to the two disciples reveals that other women were with her when she went to the tomb.

The Jewish leaders had asked Pilate to seal the tomb and put guards there to watch it for three days in case Jesus' disciples came to steal the body and then say that Jesus rose from the dead. There is evidence to believe that there may have been several Roman soldiers at the tomb (Matthew 27:63-66).

Right away, Peter and John ran together as fast as they could to see if what Mary had told them was true.

John got to the tomb before Peter. He stooped down at the entrance—and saw the linen cloths that had been wrapped around Jesus. But he didn't go in.

Peter was right behind him.

But he didn't stop at the entrance. Instead, he went right in. He saw the linen cloths that Joseph of Arimathea and Nicodemus had wrapped around Jesus' body and head. But the body was not there. The cloths were in the same position as they would have been had Jesus' body still been there. ▨

Then John went into the tomb, too. When he looked at the burial cloths again, he knew right away that Jesus had risen from the dead. ▨ He must have known that if the body had been stolen, the cloths would have been taken with the body or would have been scattered on the ground.

But Peter and John didn't stay at the tomb. Instead, they went back to their house. ▨

Joseph of Arimathea and Nicodemus used a very large amount of spices (75 pounds) to prepare Jesus' body for burial. In Jesus' time spices—myrrh and aloes—were mixed with olive oil to make a paste or ointment, and this ointment was applied to the linen cloths, which were wrapped around the body. This ointment stiffened burial cloths. So, it's possible that after the resurrection the cloths used for Jesus' burial held the shape of his body (John 19:38-40).

John tells us that John and Peter didn't think about the verses in Scripture that could be related to Jesus' crucifixion and resurrection. But John knew from what he saw that Jesus had risen from the dead (John 20:9).

Here are possible reasons why these two disciples left the tomb so quickly:
▨ They may have been fearful that if the authorities (either Roman or Jewish) found them there they would think that they had stolen the body.
▨ They may have not known exactly what to do, since they didn't know where Jesus might be.

Matthew, Mark, and Luke each present some different details, as the various witnesses experienced the scene differently. Details include a great earthquake and an angel rolling back the tomb stone, the tomb guards shaking and becoming like dead men when they saw the angel, a young man in a long white garment, and two men in shining garments. (Matthew 28:2; Mark 16:5; Luke 24:4)

Jesus' Treatment of Women: See page 9.

WHAT CAN YOU DO?

People may say that being raised from death is impossible. But the Bible teaches us that there is nothing impossible to God. Jesus proved this. He raised himself as well as at least three other people from death—the son of the widow from Nain, Jairus' daughter, and Lazarus. Jesus taught the importance of loving God with all the heart and mind and soul. And that means not giving any power or place to anything unlike God. Each day can be a great adventure in learning to see what is true about yourself and others as God's perfect, spiritual children instead of as matter bodies. You can hold good, spiritual ideas in thought. As you do, you'll be building your ability to destroy beliefs that you are sick or sinful or dying. You can rise a little each day in understanding the reality of God, Spirit, who is your life. Resurrection is every day!

Mary, on the other hand, came back to the tomb and stood there, sobbing and crying out with grief. She knelt down to look into the tomb, and saw what appeared to be two angels in white clothing. ■ Mary heard them say to her, "Woman, why are you crying?"

And she replied, "Because my Lord has been taken away, and I don't know where they have put him."

Then, she turned and looked back. She saw someone standing there. It was Jesus—but Mary didn't recognize him. Jesus said to her, "**Woman, why are you crying** like this? Who are you looking for?" Mary thought he was the person who took care of the garden.

She said to him, "Sir, if you are the one who took him, tell me where you have put him, and I will come and get him."

"Rabboni" is another word for "rabbi." Both are Hebrew words meaning "teacher."

Teacher/Master: See page 18.

The word "ascending" means "rising up," "going from a lower to a higher level." Forty days after Jesus' resurrection, the disciples were with Jesus when he rose above all thought of life as material. His understanding of Spirit and spiritual life was so complete that the disciples, who were more material in their thinking, could see him no more. He had disappeared from their sight (Mark 16:19; Luke 24:51; Acts 1:9).

Matthew says that Jesus told Mary not to be afraid. She was to tell the disciples that they should go to Galilee because that is where they would see him (Matthew 28:10).

Mary was chosen to take this message to Jesus' disciples. Most people believed that women were not as important as men. So Mary may have been afraid to speak out to the disciples. But because of what Jesus told her, she must have realized that she was not a helpless woman. She knew she could do what Jesus asked her to do.

Jesus spoke to her again. He said, "Mary!" When she heard him call her by name, she knew it was Jesus! She turned toward him and said to him, "Rabboni," meaning **Teacher.**

Mary may have reached out to cling to him. Jesus said to her, "Don't hold on to me." She was trying to hold on to him as a person. He said, "I'm still ascending." Jesus hadn't yet risen completely above material thinking and life—but his final ascension was coming soon. While he was still with her, he wanted her to be more spiritual in her thinking and not to depend on him personally to help her. She could depend on God.

Next, Jesus told her, "Go to the disciples—my brothers—and tell them I am ascending unto my Father and your Father, and to my God and your God." Jesus loved the disciples and wanted them to know he thought of them as brothers. His Father was also theirs. And their Father was with them forever to love and help them.

For to be carnally minded is death; but to be spiritually minded is life and peace.

Romans 8:6

Jesus proved by healing and by raising people from the dead how powerful spiritual thinking and prayer are. Jesus was always praying, knowing with all his might and his being, that God, Spirit, is the only reality or power. He knew that to be materially minded leads to sickness, sin, and death. But to be spiritually minded—having faith in God, Spirit—leads to health and life. Daily he went about doing good— healing others by keeping his thought filled with love, goodness, purity, harmony, health. Each day he was obedient to His Father-Mother God, turning his thought away from what he saw with his eyes and accepting instead, only spiritual perfection and the power of God. Always knowing what was spiritually true prepared him for his resurrection. His resurrection helps us see that we, too, can know the joy of life that knows no death—a life of peace and joy and power.

Mary was an obedient and loving disciple. She must have been filled with joy to do what Jesus asked her to do. How happy and grateful she must have been to share with the disciples the amazing things she saw and heard. This day was a day of wonder for them all. Their Teacher had risen from the dead!

Jesus had told them he would rise on the third day after his crucifixion and yet they had not understood that this would really happen. With his spiritual understanding of God's power and love, their Teacher had overcome death and risen from the grave. His resurrection was also theirs. He had lifted their thought higher so they could see that death could be overcome and that life is eternal.

Jesus was leaving a wonderful group of disciples—men and women. But he wasn't leaving them alone. They had the Christ—a new understanding of their spiritual selfhood—to comfort and guide them. With this understanding they would follow him by healing and bringing people back to life. Jesus expected us today to follow him, too.

Bibliography

GENERAL

Deen, Edith. *All of The Women of The Bible*. San Francisco: Harper & Row, 1955.

Eddy, Mary Baker. *Prose Works other than Science and Health with Key to the Scriptures*. Boston: The First Church of Christ, Scientist, 1953.

Eddy, Mary Baker. *Science and Health with Key to the Scriptures*. Boston: The First Church of Christ, Scientist, 1934.

Harris, Stephen L. *The New Testament, A Student's Introduction*. Mountain View: Mayfield, 1995.

Kee, Howard Clark, Young, Franklin W., Froehlich, Karlfried. *Understanding The New Testament*. Englewood Cliffs: Prentice-Hall, 1965.

Mann, Thomas W. *The Book of the Torah*. Atlanta: John Knox, 1988.

Robinson, Russell D. *Teaching the Scriptures*. Milwaukee: Bible Study, 1993.

Sergio, Lisa. *Jesus and Woman*. McLean: EPM, 1975.

Trench, Richard C. *Notes on the Miracles of Our Lord*. Grand Rapids: Baker, 1949.

Trueblood, Elton. *The Humor of Christ*. San Francisco: Harper & Row, 1964.

BIBLES

Amplified Bible. Grand Rapids: Zondervan, 1965.

Gaus, Andy. *The Unvarnished New Testament*. Grand Rapids: Phanes, 1991.

Good News Bible, The Bible in Today's English Version. Nashville: Thomas Nelson, 1976.

The Living Bible. Wheaton: Tyndale, 1976.

Hastings, Selina. *The Children's Illustrated Bible*. New York: DK, 1994.

The Holy Bible. Authorized King James Version. New York: Oxford University.

The Illustrated Family Bible. Edited by Claude-Bernard Costecalde. New York: DK, 1997.

New Jerusalem Bible. New York: Doubleday, 1990.

New Living Translation. Wheaton: Tyndale, 1996.

New International Version. Wheaton: Tyndale, 1984.

Peterson, Eugene H. *The Message*. Colorado Springs: Navpress, 1995.

Phillips, J.B. *The New Testament in Modern English*. New York: Macmillan, 1972.

DICTIONARIES AND CONCORDANCES

The Anchor Bible Dictionary. Edited by David Noel Freedman. New York: Doubleday, 1992.

Dictionary of Judaism in the Biblical Period. Edited by Jacob Neusner. Peabody: Hendrickson, 1966.

Dictionary of the Bible. Edited by James Hastings. New York: Charles Scribner's Sons, 1963.

HarperCollins Bible Dictionary. San Francisco: Harper. 1996.

Illustrated Dictionary of Bible Life and Times. Pleasantville: Reader's Digest, 1997.

International Standard Bible Encyclopedia Electronic Edition STEP Files. Parsons Technology, 1998.

The Interpreter's Dictionary of the Bible. Edited by George Arthur Buttrick. Nashville: Abingdon, 1962.

Quick Verse for Windows Version 5.0c. Cedar Rapids: Parsons Technology, 1992-1998:

> *Holman Bible Dictionary.* Edited by Trent C. Butler.
> *International Standard Bible Encyclopedia.* Edited by James Orr, 1998.

Strong, James. *The Exhaustive Concordance of The Bible.* Nashville: Abingdon, 1980.

Thayer, Joseph H. *Thayer's Greek-English Lexicon of the New Testament.* Grand Rapids: Baker, 1977.

COMMENTARIES

Barclay, William. *The Daily Study Bible.* Philadelphia: Westminster, 1975.

A Commentary on The Holy Bible. Edited by Rev. J.R. Dummelow. New York: Macmillan, 1939.

The Expositor's Bible Commentary. Edited by Frank E. Gaebelein. Grand Rapids: Zondervan, 1984.

Harper's Bible Commentary. Edited by James L. Mays. San Francisco: Harper & Row, 1988.

The Interpreter's Bible. Nashville: Abingdon, 1982.

The Interpreter's One-Volume Commentary on the Bible. Edited by Charles M. Laymon. Nashville: Abingdon, 1971.

JFB Commentary on The Whole Bible. Edited by Robert Jamieson, A.E. Fausset, David Brown. Grand Rapids: Zondervan, 1961.

Henry, Matthew. *Matthew Henry's Commentary on the Whole Bible.* New York: Fleming H. Revell.

The New Interpreter's Bible. Edited by Leander E. Keck. Nashville: Abingdon, 1995.

Stern, David S. *Jewish New Testament Commentary.* Clarksville, MD: Jewish New Testament Publications, Inc. 1995.

The Tyndale New Testament Commentaries. Edited by Canon Leon Morris. Grand Rapids: William B. Eerdmans, 1985.

The Wycliffe Bible Commentary. Edited by Everett G. Harrison. Nashville: Southwestern, 1962.

ATLASES

Atlas of the Bible Lands. Edited by Harry Thomas Frank. Maplewood, NJ: Hammond, 1990.

Oxford Bible Atlas. Edited by Herbert G. May. London: Oxford University, 1976.

DAILY LIFE IN BIBLE TIMES

Connolly, Peter. *Living in the Time of Jesus of Nazareth.* Israel: Steimatzky, 1983.

Derrett, J. Duncan M. *Jesus's Audience.* New York: Seabury, 1973.

Gower, Ralph. *The New Manners and Customs of Bible Times.* Chicago: Moody Press, 1987.

Great People of the Bible and How They Lived. Pleasantville: Reader's Digest, 1974.

Harper's Encyclopedia of Bible Life. Madeleine S. and J. Lane Miller. Edison: Castle, 1978.

Jesus and His Times. Edited by Kaari Ward. Pleasantville: Reader's Digest, 1987.

Thompson, J.A. *Handbook of Life in Bible Times.* Madison: Inter-Varsity, 1986.

Index to "What Can YOU Do?" Sidebars

Below are listed the "concerns" addressed in sidebars.

Index to Bible Verses

With this index, you will be able to find Bible verses in the stories and sidebars. In some cases, the Bible verses are paraphrased, rather than quoted or referenced. Bible books, chapters, and verses below are in the left column and in bold type. Page numbers are to the right of the verses. Page numbers in bold type indicate this verse is the subject of a sidebar.

General Index